COOPER FINDS HER THERMAL

AS TOLD TO GEORGE MILLER BY A LITTLE PINK BIRD

How did this Miller clown get his name on my book?

Read your contract.

ISBN: 978-1-7332326-4-7
Manufactured in the United States
First Edition

Copyright © 2022
by George Miller

Millstone Publishing
Friendship, Maryland 20758

Miller, George 1945
Cooper Finds Her Thermal p. cm.
Includes design, images, graphics, and photos by Donald Shomette
Bird photography by Carol Frost and George Miller; Narrative by George Miller

My job is to save the wilderness.
I don't know anything else worth saving.
— Edward Abbey,
The Monkey Wrench Gang

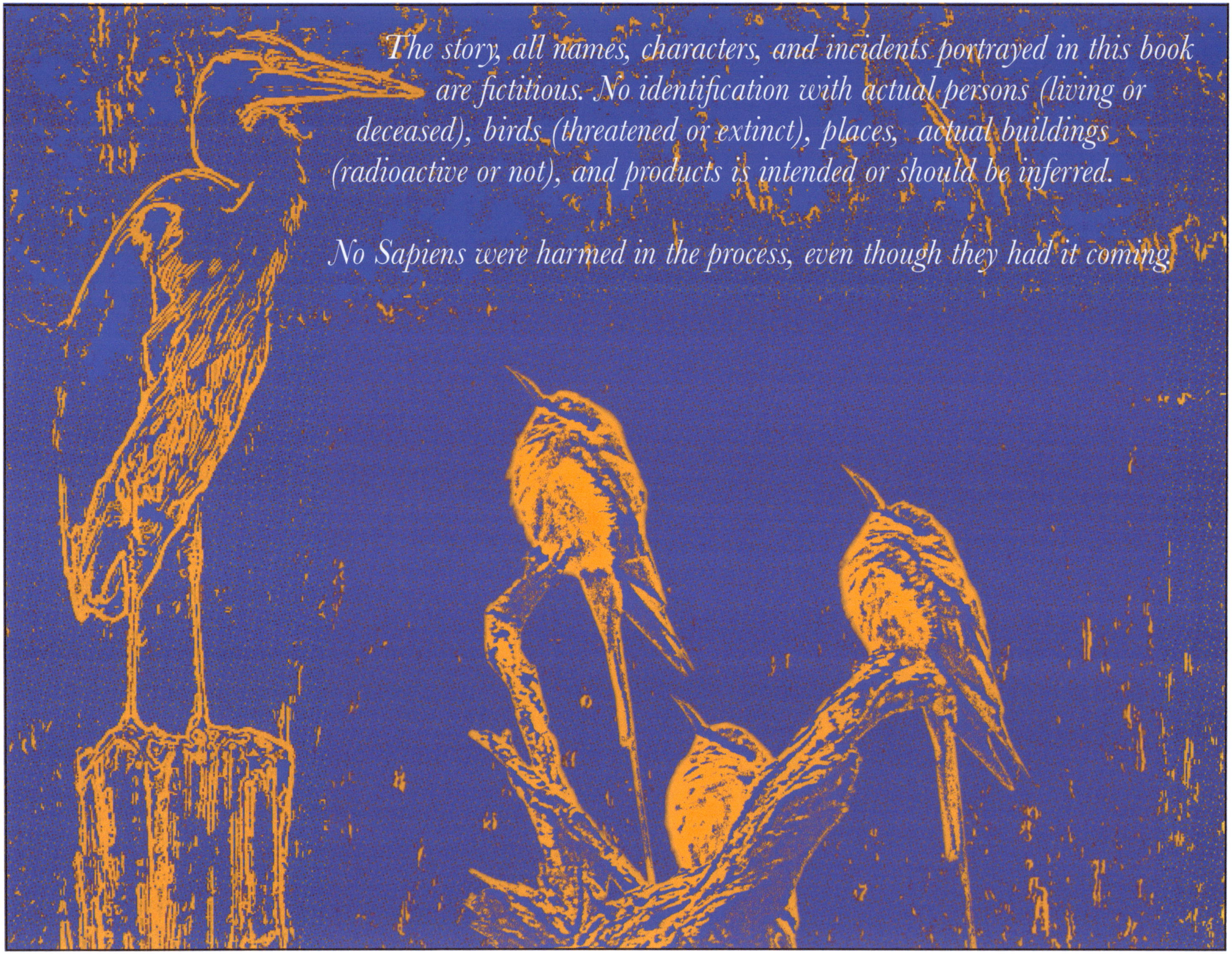

The story, all names, characters, and incidents portrayed in this book are fictitious. No identification with actual persons (living or deceased), birds (threatened or extinct), places, actual buildings (radioactive or not), and products is intended or should be inferred.

No Sapiens were harmed in the process, even though they had it coming.

Cooper has her mother's eyes

1

Pick on somebody your own size

Hawk Eyes Can Spot a Baby Blue Bird Miles Away

PREDATOR

Hawks are birds of prey.

That's Cooper's niche.

Her niche has a
bad name.

Cooper doesn't
understand predation,
far too many syllables
for a young hawk.

*What's
to
understand?
You
catch
them.
You eat
them.
Fair?*

3

COOPER AND
HER MOTHER
LIVED HAPPILY IN
THEIR SUMMER
HOME ALONG
THE
SUSQUEHANNA
RIVER IN
CENTRAL
PENNSYLVANIA

*Where's the dad? Why's it
always the mom stuck
home with the fledglings?*

THEIR COMFORTABLE
LIFE STYLE REVOLVED
AROUND PREDATION
AND THE GOOEY BITES
HER MOTHER FED HER

*Who
could
ask
for
more?*

*I have
a bad feeling
about this.*

5

I can't watch this.

Never cross the Avian Legion
of Decency. Didn't you learn
that when we banned
your last book?

Maybe we should cut this scene, a little
too graphic for our pusillanimous,
pussy-footing censors.

ONE OVERCAST
AUTUMN DAY,
MOTHER HAWK
KICKED COOPER
OUT OF THE NEST
WITHOUT
ANY WARNING

Time to grow up, Baby.

Why'd you do that?

"I'm off to see my boyfriend at his winter home in Florida"

said Mother Hawk before she snowbirded effortlessly into the sky.

Miami Beach - 1242

Doesn't look effortlessly to me.

8

Mother Hawk
Circled Around
Once More

Find
your
thermal.
It will serve
you well.

What's a thermal?

Miami Beach - 12

Wings to fly and all that.

I studied thermals in
high school physics,
something
about hot air.

This thermal thing is so confusing.

HOOT OWL EXPLAINED THE SCIENCE

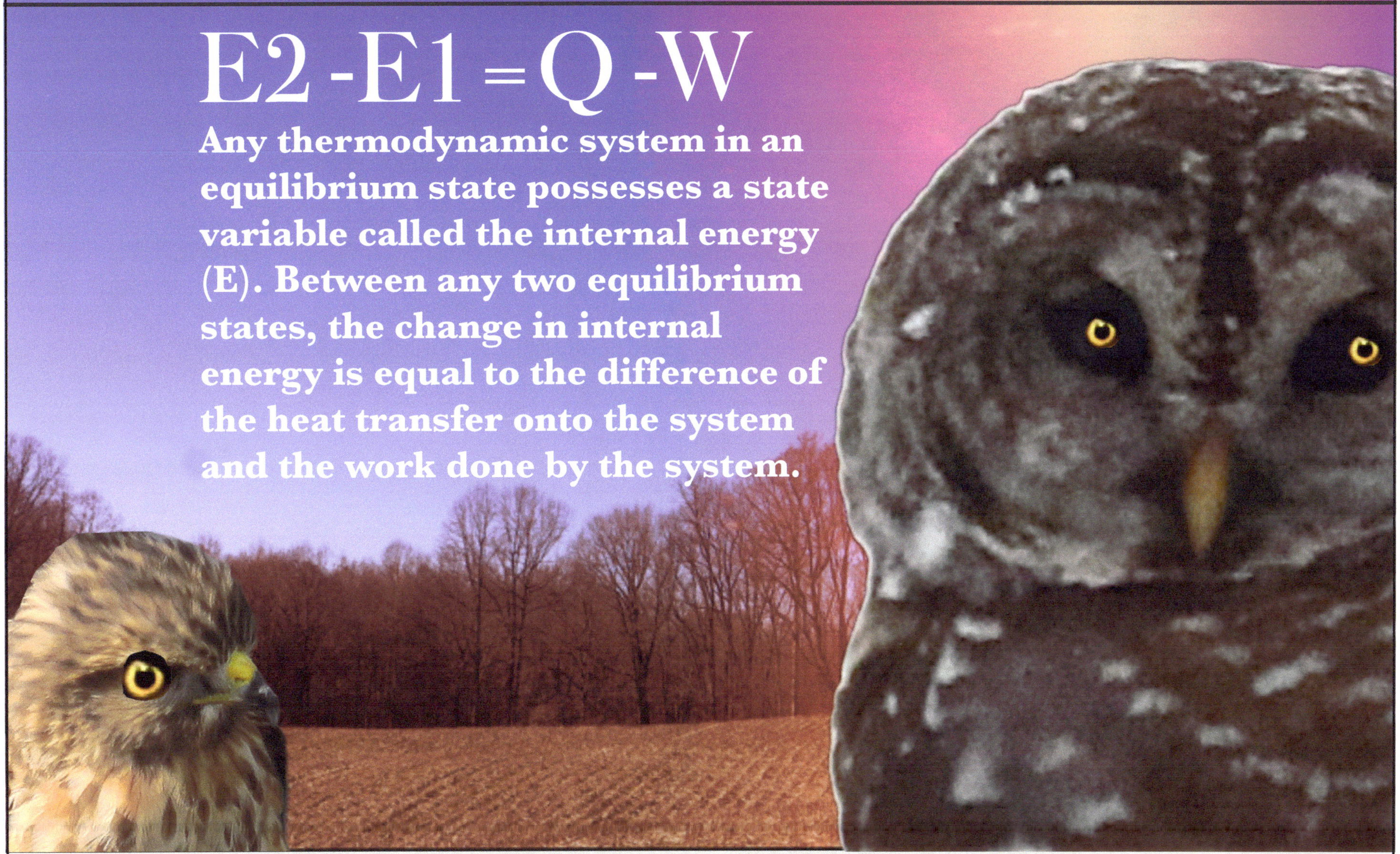

$$E2 - E1 = Q - W$$

Any thermodynamic system in an equilibrium state possesses a state variable called the internal energy (E). Between any two equilibrium states, the change in internal energy is equal to the difference of the heat transfer onto the system and the work done by the system.

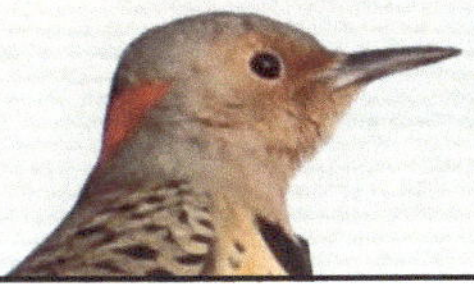

The first law of thermodynamics, if I'm not mistaken.

Might be a bit over her head.

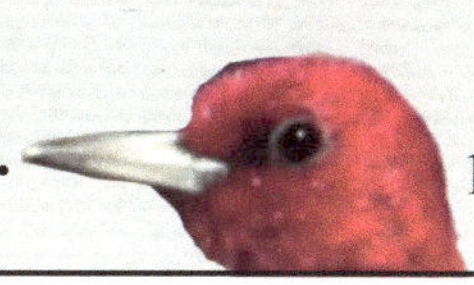

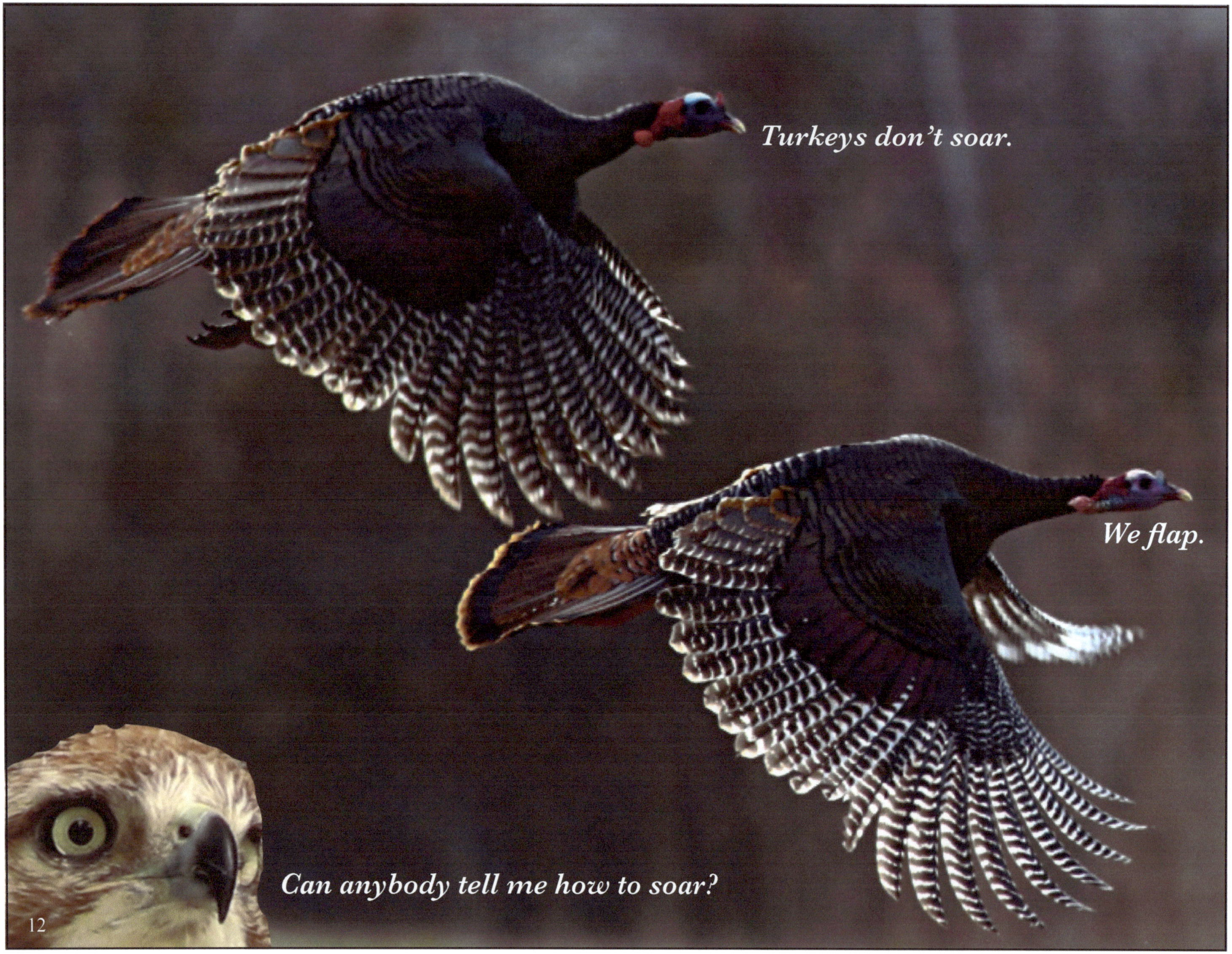

Turkeys don't soar.

We flap.

Can anybody tell me how to soar?

We kettle around in giant circles, never know when we'll find our wave.

Sorry, gotta run, there's our thermal now, the 5:02 from the Gulf of Mexico.

♪♪♪♪♪

Off to Alaska …

Kettle, Smettle! How do I find my mother? I'm hungry.

13

OUT OF THE BLUE,
A BOXCAR SIZED
WOOD STORK
BANKED IN FROM
FLORIDA

I just caught
a rogue thermal
from Corkscrew
to Central
Pennsylvania.

WAHOOOO !!!

Take a
gander
at the
wingspan
on that
beast.

Must be
sort of
mutant.

Are you my father?

EAGLES DON'T SEE THERMALS, WE FEEL THEM

Some day my thermal will come

And the warblers will warble

MEANWHILE, BACK AT THE "AROUND THE CANOPY" TALK SHOW

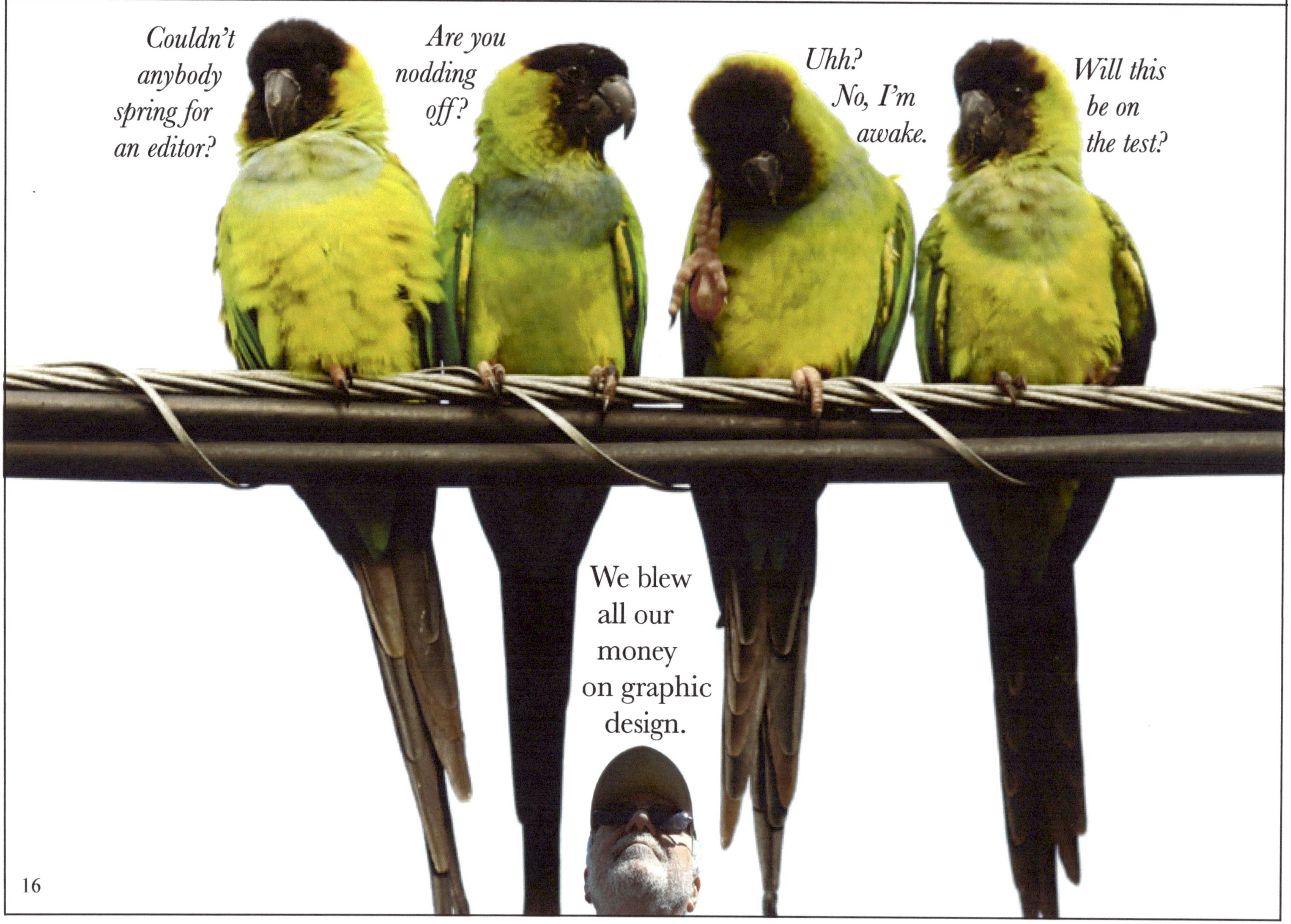

Couldn't anybody spring for an editor?
Are you nodding off?
Uhh? No, I'm awake.
Will this be on the test?
We blew all our money on graphic design.

PSSSST !! Your plot is a smidgen slow. Would you like to juice it up with a pirated story line? I'll let it go for $5000.

$1500 and nobody gets hurt. That's my bottom line.

I have a client, a nobody graphic novelist, a total guano. It's not even his story, probably picked it up in the canopy. Let's say $3000.

$3000 for a parroted pirated story line?

He's only a name-dropping woodpecker. $2000 and only the woodpecker gets hurt. Deal?

Deal! As long as I don't get caught. That's my bottom line.

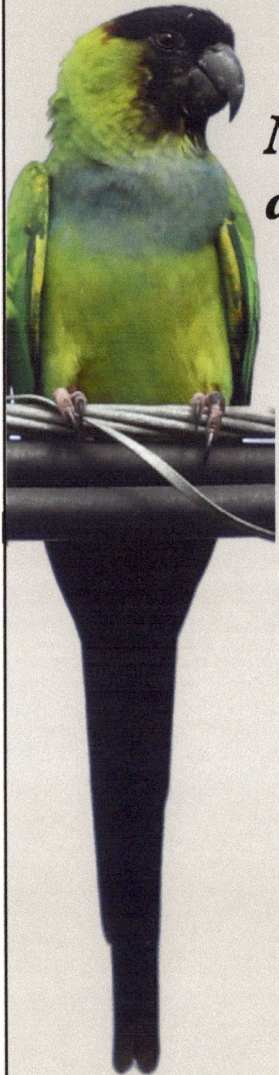

Now for the juiced up story line, definite Pulitzer potential.

WARNING
CLEVER PLOT
TWIST AHEAD
STAY ALERT

A Cooper's Hawk, a rebel in the Avian Apocalypse, abandoned by her mother at an early age, makes the perilous journey from Pennsylvania to Florida with the aid of her fellow wing-farers: a vulture, an owl, and a little pink bird. In a clever plot twist, they align behind the Assateague Avian Accord to annihilate the Headwater Dam and the Chesapeake Nuclear Power Plant.

Annihilation, apocalyptic, intrigue, abandonment, parental conflict, and a little pink bird. You're talking to the master of clever plot twists.

This clever plot twist sounds familiar.

Something Olde, Something New, Something Borrowed, Something Blue

COOPER FLAPPED
HER WINGS AS HARD
AS HER LITTLE HAWK
HEART WAS ABLE.
ALL SHE FELT WAS
THE BRANCH
BENEATH HER
TALONS

I give an "E" for effort.

Or "D" for dead.

SHE FLAPPED
AND FLAPPED
UNTIL SHE
COLLAPSED

19

I can't
watch
this.

YUM, *Road Kill*

20

TURKEY VULTURE TOUCHED DOWN FOR A CLOSER LOOK

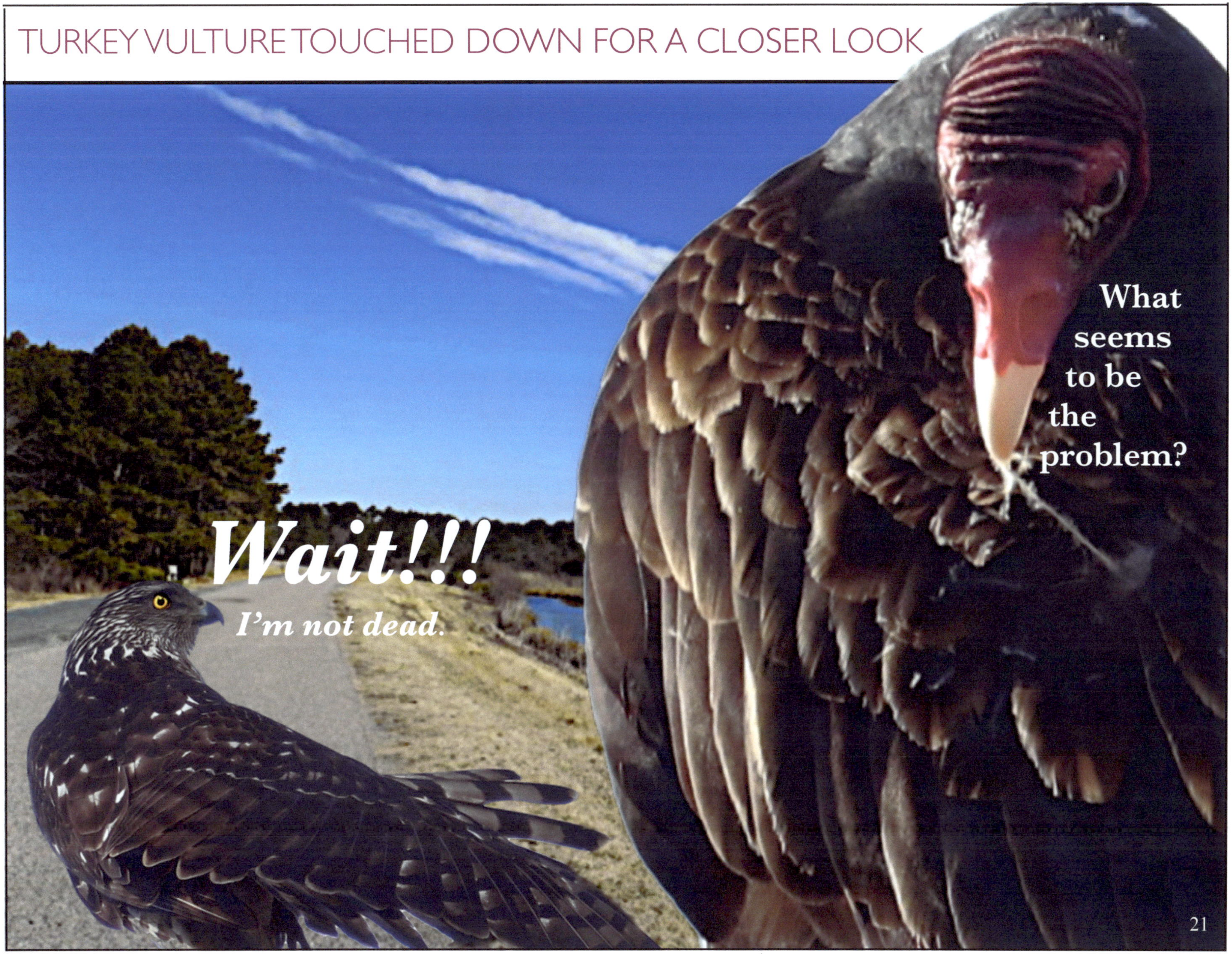

Can you
speak a
smidgen
SLOWER?

My mother flew off to Florida without me. I need to find my thermal, but I don't know how. How do I feel the wind beneath my wings?

I feel the wind ... 🎵🎵🎵

MENTOR THAT SHE WAS, TURKEY VULTURE
HOPPED ON A NEARBY TREE BRANCH
AND SPREAD HER WINGS

And off she glided, up and away.

COOPER JUMPED ON THE DEAD TREE BRANCH AND SPREAD HER WINGS

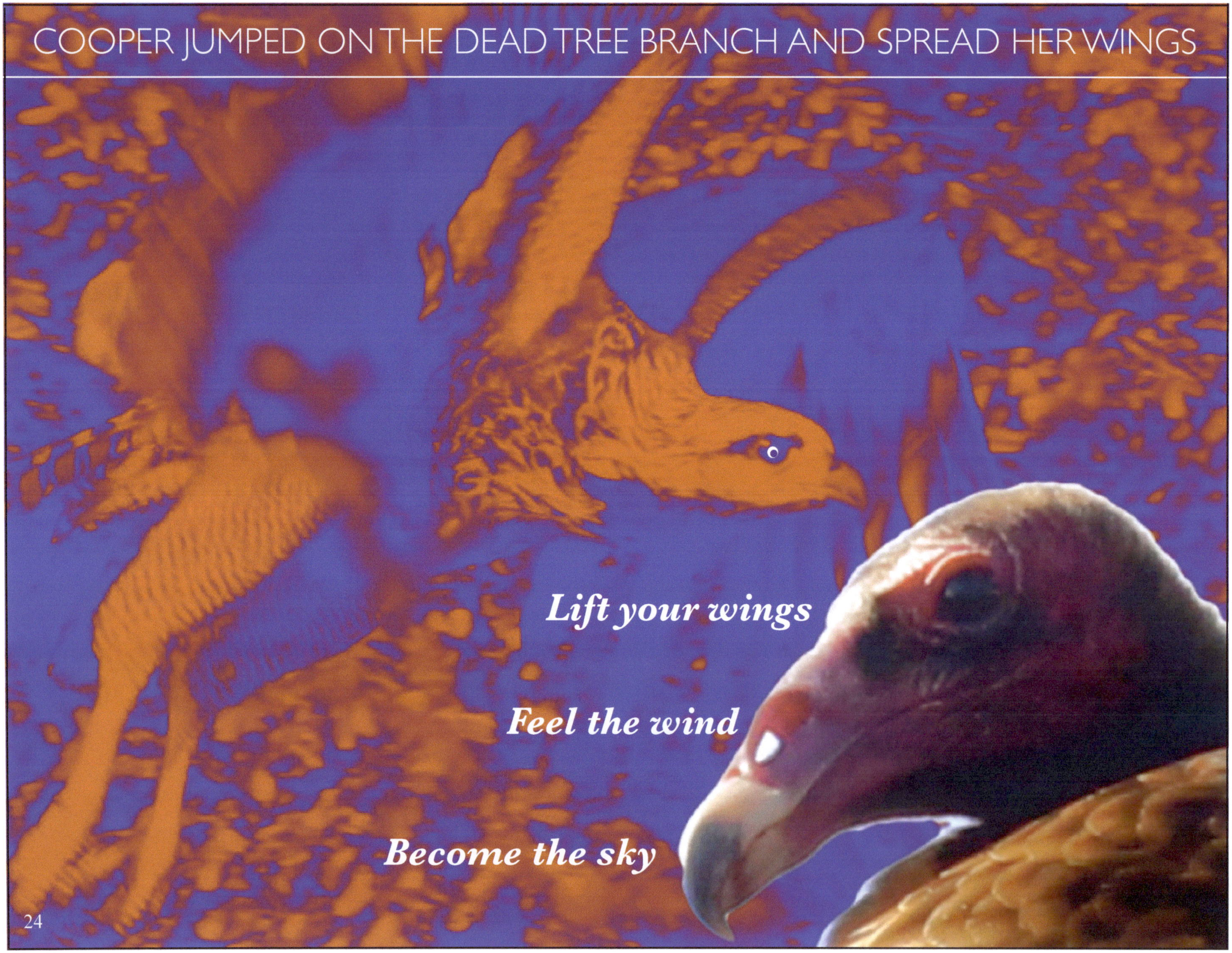

Lift your wings

Feel the wind

Become the sky

*Now,
off
to
find
my
mother !!*

Look there, up in the air.

It's a plane.

It's Super Cooper.

It's a bird.

COASTAL MIGRATION ROUTE

By my calculations, your mother should be flying over Cape May about now.

Cape May

And how do I get to Cape May?

We take the coastal thermal.

Mom! Wait for me !!

I give her an 'S' for spunk.

Are we grading on the curve again?

27

Look,
a Cooper's
Hawk,
very
dangerous,
eats
song birds.

Has anybody seen my mother?
18 inches long, a blue-gray back,
reddish bars on her belly, a black
cap, and dark bands on her tail.

WE'RE IN DEEP GUANO!

Maybe if we help
her find her mother,
she won't eat us.

THE CAPE MAY
HAWK WATCH

A Partnership Project Sponsored by

SWAROVSKI
OPTIK

STATE PARK SERVICE
DIVISION OF PARKS
AND FORESTRY
N.J.

Good thinking,
Blue.

Your mother went that way, not more than ten minutes ago. If you hurry, you can catch her.

Ten minutes? Really?

29

Why so sad, Young Misses?

I don't have any friends.
The song birds think I'll eat them.

Do you want to talk about it?

Who could possibly help?

We can ask Hoot Owl.
She'll know what to do.

Can she solve predator problems?

Absolutely,
she helped me with my
roadkill disorder.

30

My friend Cooper has a problem.
She frightens song birds.
They're afraid
she'll eat them.

Turkey Vulture,
what brings
you to my
doorstep?

I typically put
my young hawks
on a diet of
moles, voles,
and shrews.

Anything without a soul.

What's a soul?

31

All well and good, but how do I find my mother?

The Sapiens are up to no good again, something about sediment load recalibration.

You can tag along with us. We're headed to an emergency meeting of the Avian Environmental Conference at the Headwater Dam. Some of the best and brightest bird brains will be there.

Best and brightest? Why weren't we invited?

There's a lot of woodpecker bias around these days.

This sediment load thing is so confusing.

Can you believe it? 50,000 tons of contaminated sludge backed up behind the Headwater Dam, coal-black muck, cow crap, pig crap, chicken crap, Sapiens crap, heavy metals, pharmaceuticals, and agrochemical fertilizers, an existential threat. Who's going to pay for this? Sister Crab! Sister Oyster! That's who!

33

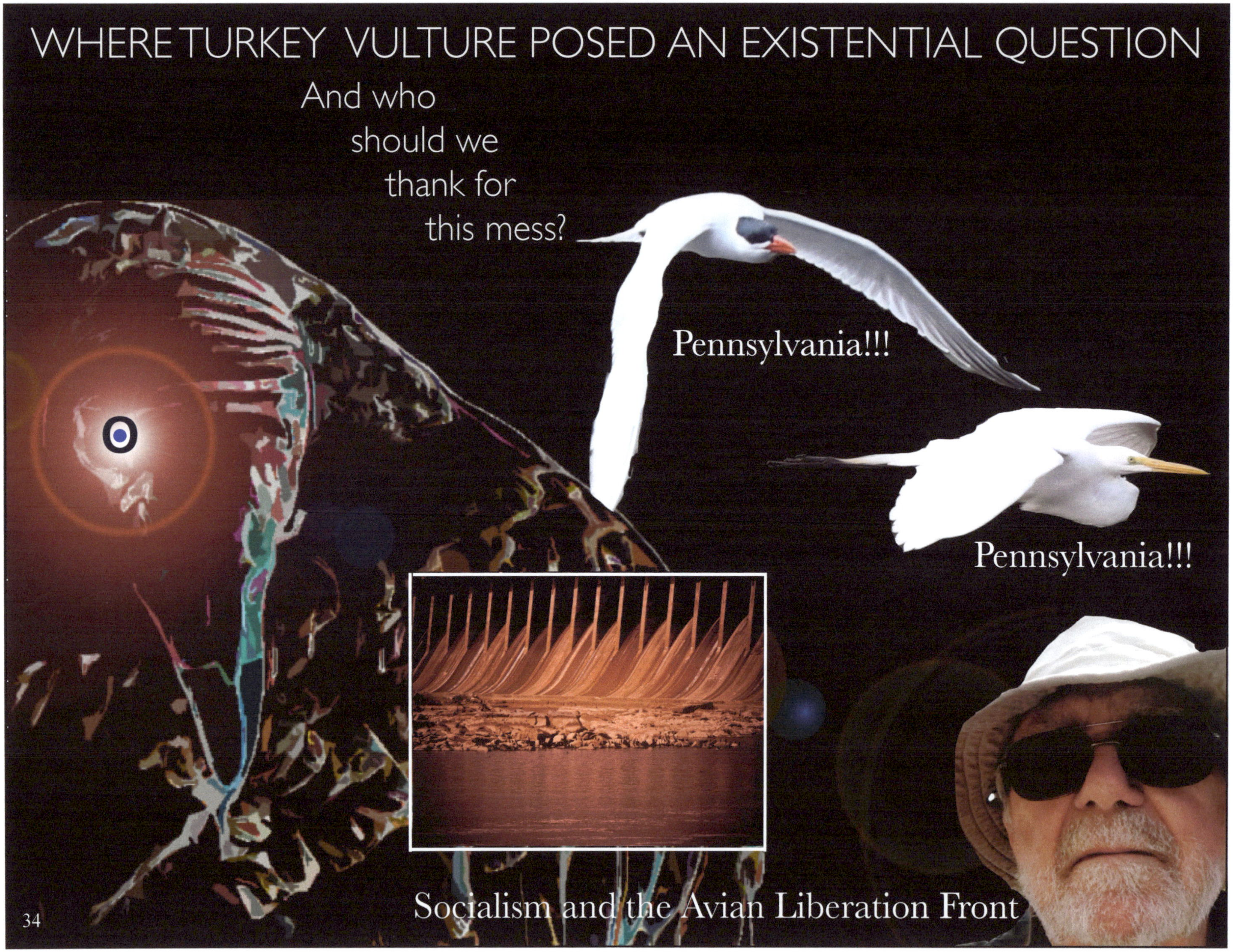
WHERE TURKEY VULTURE POSED AN EXISTENTIAL QUESTION
And who should we thank for this mess?
Pennsylvania!!!
Pennsylvania!!!
Socialism and the Avian Liberation Front

When do
we catch
up with
my mother ?

COASTAL
MIGRATION
ROUTE

We can't be too
far behind her.
Let's check the
Western Shore.
Does she play
the slots?
Maybe
Chesapeake
Beach?

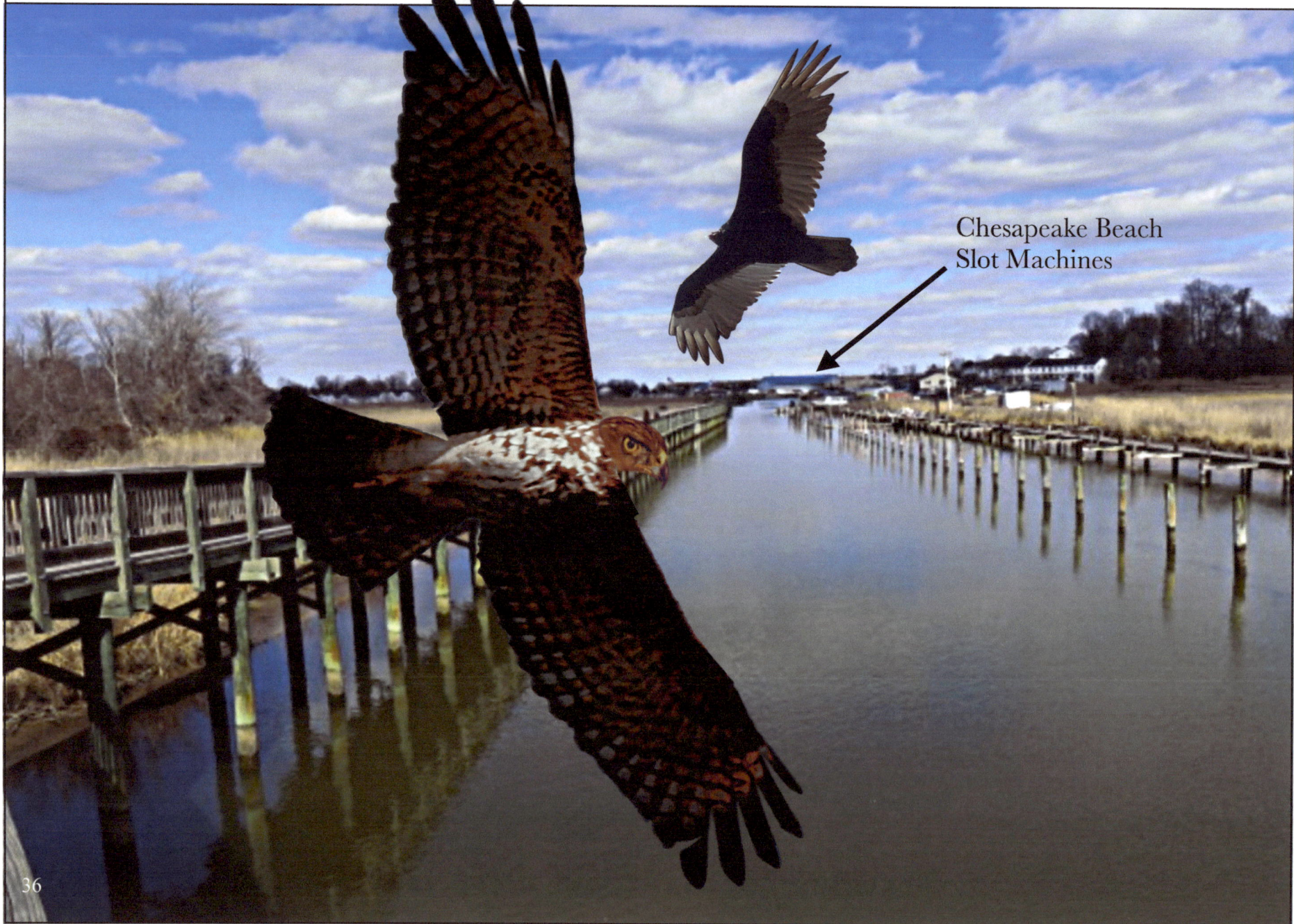

Chesapeake Beach
Slot Machines

36

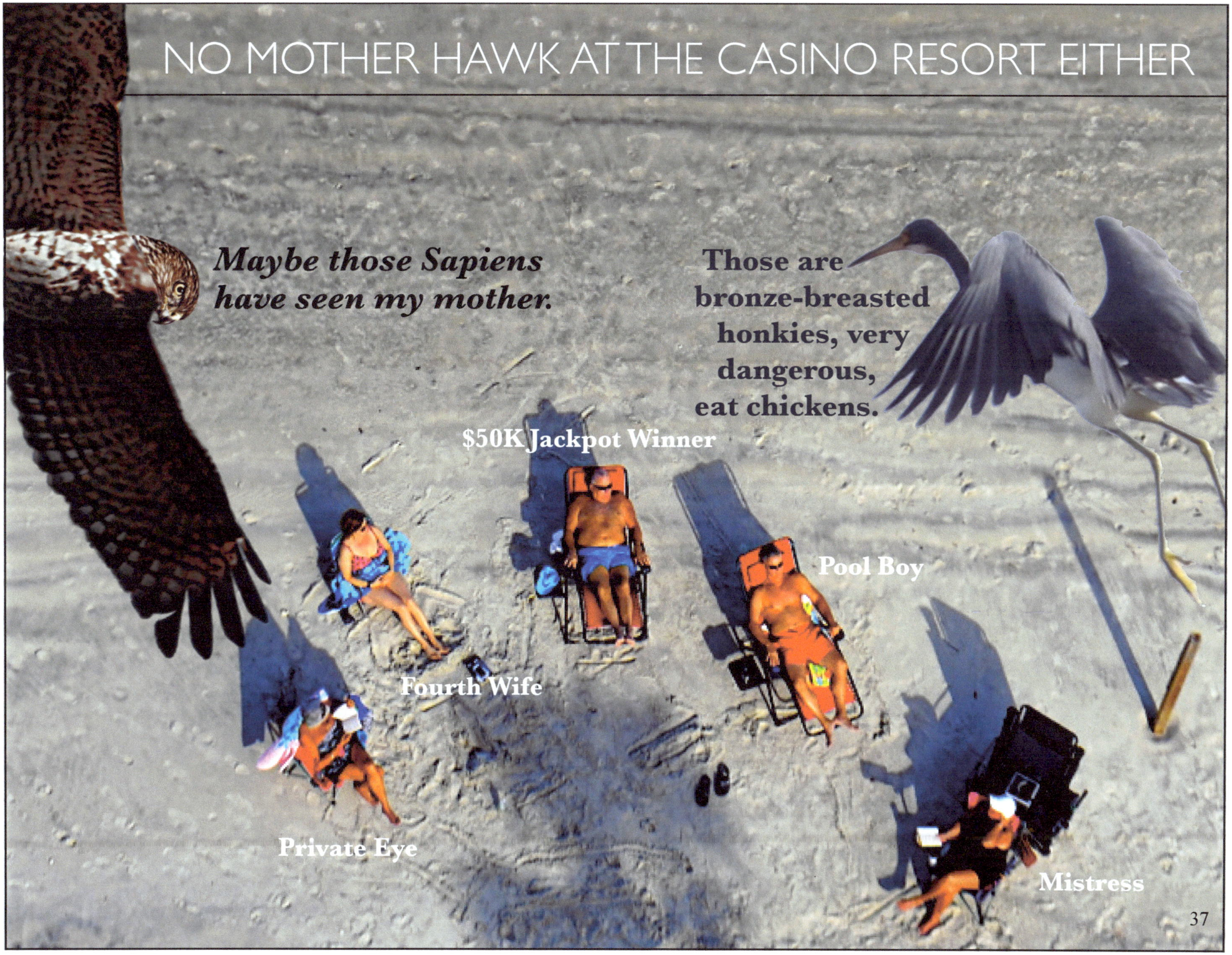
NO MOTHER HAWK AT THE CASINO RESORT EITHER
Maybe those Sapiens have seen my mother.
Those are bronze-breasted honkies, very dangerous, eat chickens.
$50K Jackpot Winner
Pool Boy
Fourth Wife
Private Eye
Mistress

Sapiens felled hundreds of thousands
of perfectly good nesting trees
to build hundreds of warships,
then sank them in the river.

That's a lot
of woodpecker holes
down the tubes.

Just ask Sister
Ivory-bill.
May she rest in peace.

38

PSSSST !! Missed opportunity here, try something feminine: motherhood, fledglings, nesting.

Fledglings, nesting, motherhood, sensitivity? How hard can that be?

Think sides of the brain, right side, feminine, artistic, left side, male, analytical. Got it?

Got it !!

I'm not sure this nonsense applies to bird brains.

I'm not sure it applies to anything.

39

ONCE MORE WITH FEELING

That ghostly boat looks like a good place to raise my fledglings.

Excellent character development, brings out the mother in our heroine.

PSSSST !!

These know-it-all parakeets are subverting our environmental statement into a sappy love story.

I signed on to become an eco-terrorist.

I just want to find my mother.

Rumble in the Marsh,
Sapiens versus Avians,
that's the way I see it.

I thought my book was about thermodynamic lift, the thrill to be aloft, wings to fly, all that.

Cooper, I've been expecting you. Turkey Vulture said you might pass our way.

Where is she? I'm overdue for my thermal lesson.

42

Turkey Vulture and Hoot Owl headed down the shore line. Something about an emergency at the Nuclear Power Plant.

Emergency?

Are they hurt?

They can take care of themselves, but we're still worried about them.

I'm on my way!!

Does anyone else notice that it feels a bit warm around here?

BELCH!

Check out Reactor 2. Now that's what I call a thermal!

SHE'S GONNA BLOW!

A forty-five-year license renewal for the Chesapeake Nuclear Power Plant. We're stuck with this radioactive behemoth until 2062, decades of spent fuel onsite, a dry cask storage facility on the Chesapeake, a ticking time bomb.

Tick

Tick

Tick

Tick

Tick

Tick

Tick

Tick

China
8000 Miles

Receding Shore
Line - 150 Yards

E=MC^2

Tick
Tick
Tick
Tick
Tick

August 6, 1945

Fukushima Daiichi, Three Mile Island, and Chernobyl, if my memory serves.

Does everybody around this place have a short memory?

Sorry, I don't remember.

I'm here to assure you
there is no danger
of radiation leakage
or contaminated muck
as the left wing Avians
would have you believe.
The Chesapeake is safe
for generations to come.

*Are you a
good vulture
or a bad
vulture?*

47

What's to be done?

We organize, that's what we do!

How? What could possibly work?

An Accord, like Port Huron,
but flightier.

I'm with you on that, Sister.

Wait a minute, I got it, the
Assateague Avian Accord.

Alliterative, I like it.

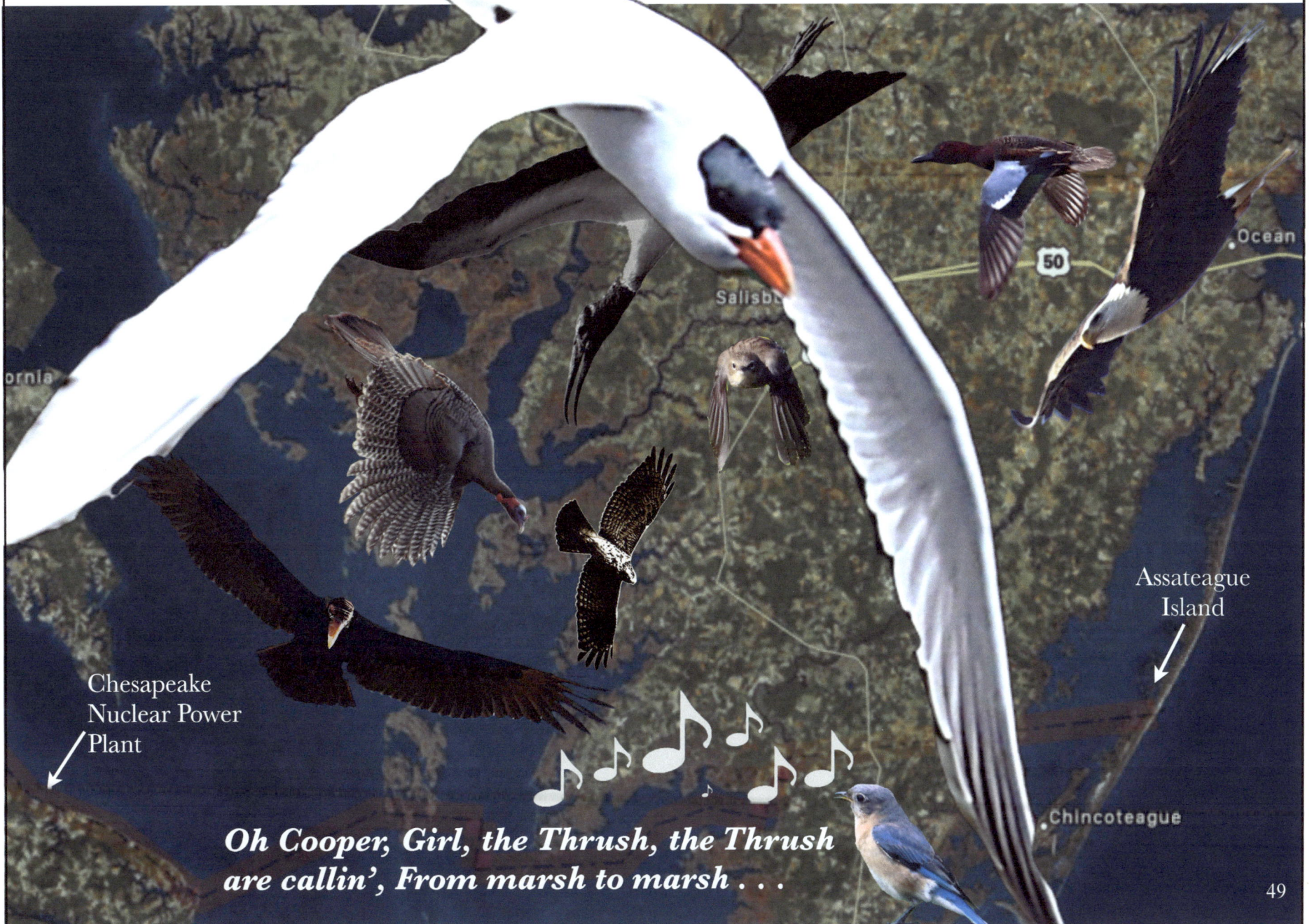

Chesapeake
Nuclear Power
Plant

Assateague
Island

Oh Cooper, Girl, the Thrush, the Thrush
are callin', From marsh to marsh . . .

Tourists! Who needs them?

Isn't that Amy of Assateague?

No, that's Jerome, a chestnut pinto stallion.

I'm a grandmother. I don't need a pontificating old male explaining the difference between a stallion and a mare.

I say we form the Monkey Wrench Flock and blow the Headwater Dam.

What about the muck? It will swamp the bay.

The sooner we can start over again, the better.

I say we storm the Eastern Shore and free the chickens.

What about us turkeys?

Bring flowers to the Revolution.

52

The Chesapeake Nuclear Reactor has to go. Save some dynamite for that.

You can't dynamite a nuclear reactor.

Why not? Sapiens drained my swamp!

Sapiens? Let me guess, they named themselves.

Don't confuse semantics with an engineering problem.

GREAT BLUE HERON STORMED THE EASTERN SHORE TO FREE THE CHICKENS

Ride of the Valkyries?

Cheap theater trick, but it still works.

ASSATEAGUE AVIAN ACCORD - DAY 5

SHORE BIRDS ACCOSTED THE CHESAPEAKE NUCLEAR POWER PLANT ON PADDLE BOARDS

Hello, this is the Provisional Avian Republic of Chesapeake. We have you surrounded. Stand down. You are hereby decommissioned.

ASSATEAGUE AVIAN ACCORD - DOOMS DAY
THE POWER GRID STRIKES BACK
Where can we get some road kill around this place?
There she is. Get her.
When do we get paid?
Never leave your wing bird.
I have her in my sights.
Surrender, Cooper !!
Never !!!!!!!!!!

*Maybe we should
shuffle Cooper
out of here.
Too many Sapiens
on her tail.*

**Good thinking, what
do you suggest?**

*Florida, a good place
to disappear.*

**And find
her mother?**

WITH THE STORM VULTURES IN HOT PURSUIT, COOPER DUCKED INTO THE OKEFENOKEE SWAMP

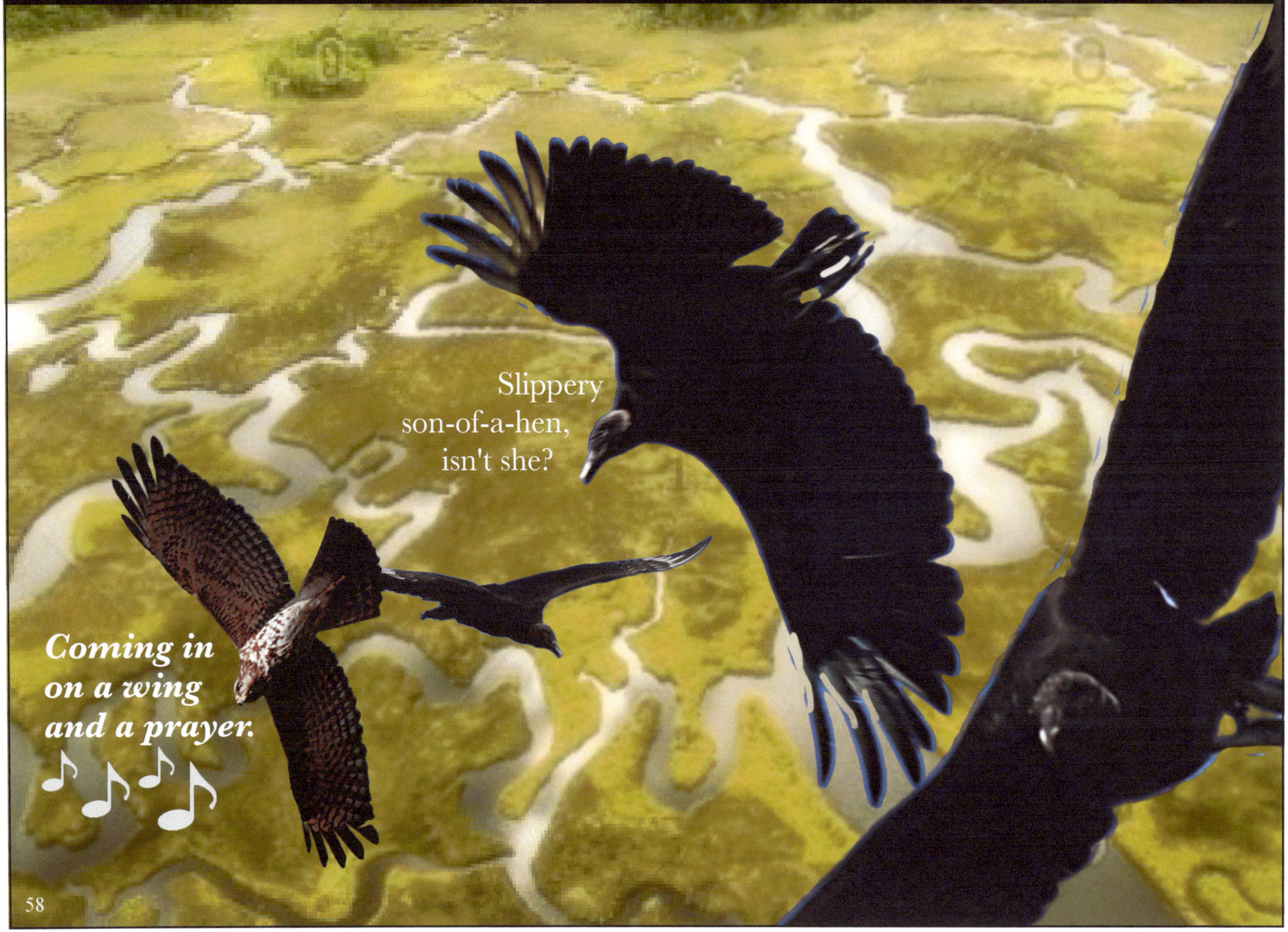
Slippery
son-of-a-hen,
isn't she?
Coming in
on a wing
and a prayer.

Lord God!
Isn't that the last
ivory-billed
woodpecker?

Correct me if
I'm wrong, but
I make that
out to be a
yellow-bellied
sapsucker.

For ivory bills you need to visit Cuba,
last sighting by Giraldo Alayon in 1987.

59

Cooper, I've been expecting you. Turkey Vulture asked me to look out for you.

Welcome to Florida?

WTF?

Florida! At last!
Now maybe I can
find my mother.
How far to Miami?

Never mind Miami. We'll hide you in the Everglades until things settle down.

COOPER
FLEW
OVER
CENTRAL
FLORIDA
WHERE
SAPIENS
SOUGHT
TO
BAN
LGBTQ
BIRDS
FROM
STATE
PARKS

Correct me if I'm wrong, but
isn't that a rainbow-pride moorhen?

The preferred term is Purple Gallinule.

*This book is totally unsuitable
for impressionable school-aged
children in the Sunshine State.*

If you're looking for a class-act mother, stop by the Fairchild Gardens in Miami. Sit a spell with Marjory Stoneman Douglas.

Come sit with me

Now, that's what I call a MOTHER

Marjory Stoneman Douglas, the Mother of the Everglades. She warms my little pink heart.

64

FROM THERE, COOPER PROCEEDED TO HER RENDEZVOUS IN THE EVERGLADES

Now, that's what I call a predator

Yum, tastes like chicken.

There's your diversion. Fly like hell.

What about the pool boy?

Collateral damage.

What about my mother?

She made her choice.

What about the earth?

Your choice.

That's the worst Groucho impersonation I've ever seen.

You bet your life.

That's the worst Hemingway impersonation I've ever seen.

I've seen worse. I studied drama at Woodpecker U.

Lark

AS LUCK
WOULD
HAVE IT,
COOPER
RAN INTO
HER MOTHER

Look at me, Mom. I can fly.

Let's go, Birdie, before
we miss the last thermal
back to South Beach.

Sorry, Cooper,
I have a date
with my
boyfriend.

Definitely not a
Hollywood
ending.

Fortunately, that's not the end of our story. The next summer Cooper followed her instincts back to Mallows Bay where she began a family as a proper mother.

The Evil Doers searched high and low in the Everglades, never suspecting that Cooper lived under their noses in Southern Maryland.

Now, that's what I call a Hollywood ending.

Pooper   Drooper   Trooper

Her friends welcomed her to her new home where she ostensibly lived happily ever after.

But, as you and I know, she lay low, formenting

R
E
V
O
L
U
T
I
O
N

♪ ♪ ♪ ♪
This marsh is my marsh.

♪ ♪ ♪ ♪
This marsh is your marsh.

Mothers are birds, too.
Wings to flap and all that.

Find your thermal.
It will serve you well.

When you
reach
the end of
the road,
remember
the
friends
who got
you there.

Don't let your clever plot
twist get caught in a wringer.

If you can't save
yourself, save the
earth for your
grandfledglings.

Don't be a pusillanimous,
pussyfooting electricity-phobe.

Did I mention, I studied ethics at Woodpecker U?

EPILOGUE

The Eastern Shore chickens cling to their prophecy for the Messianic Great Blue to deliver them from their hellacious conveyer belt.

In June 2021, the Summer Tanager Award for the best book by a little pink bird was awarded to Little Pink Bird.

Headwater Dam and the Chesapeake Nuclear Power Plant chug along, supplying power to Sapiens up and down the east coast.

Sadly, George Miller never received the Pulitzer he craved. He did receive a sketchy tax deduction for all the money he purportedly poured into this ill-advised project.

I'd like to thank my mother for teaching me that pink trumps hot air.

I'd like to thank my tax attorney for keeping me out of jail.

73

Stay tuned for our
next exciting
episode:

*RUMBLE IN
THE MARSH*

www.ingramcontent.com/pod-product-compliance
Lightning Source LLC
Chambersburg PA
CBHW041553030426
42336CB00005B/60